HAPPENINGS

Senior Authors
Carl B. Smith
Virginia A. Arnold

Linguistics Consultant
Ronald Wardhaugh

Macmillan Publishing Co., Inc.
New York

Collier Macmillan Publishers
London

This work is also published together with other works in a single volume under the title: *Rhymes and Reasons,* copyright © 1983 Macmillan Publishing Co., Inc. Parts of this work were published in earlier editions of SERIES r.

Macmillan Publishing Co., Inc.
866 Third Avenue, New York, New York 10022
Collier Macmillan Canada, Inc.

Printed in the United States of America
ISBN 0-02-132120-5
9 8 7 6 5 4 3 2

ACKNOWLEDGMENTS

The publisher gratefully acknowledges permission to reprint the following copyrighted material:

"Familiar Friends," from *Crickety Cricket! The Best-Loved Poems of James S. Tippett.* Copyright © 1973 by Martha K. Tippett. By permission of Harper & Row, Publishers, Inc. and World's Work Ltd.

"Feather or Fur," from *New Feathers For The Old Goose* by John Becker. Copyright by John Becker and reprinted with his permission.

"Hawk, I'm Your Brother," from *Hawk, I'm Your Brother* by Byrd Baylor. Copyright © 1976 by Byrd Baylor. Reprinted also by permission of Charles Scribner's Sons and Toni Strassman, Agent.

"Hurt No Living Thing," from *Sing-Song* by Christina G. Rossetti. Published by Macmillan Publishing Co., Inc., 1924.

"My Caruso," by Earl G. Robbins is printed here with his permission.

"Wilbur's Boast," selected from *Charlotte's Web* by E.B. White. Illustrations by Garth Williams. Copyright © 1952, by E.B. White. By permission of Harper & Row, Publishers, Inc. and Hamish Hamilton Ltd.

"Wufu," from *Wufu: The Story of a Little Brown Bat* by Berniece Freschet. Copyright © 1975 by Berniece Freschet. Reprinted by permission of G.P. Putnam's Sons.

Illustrations: Ray Cruz, pp. 4-7; Frank Bozzo, pp. 10-11; Garth Williams, pp. 12-23; M. (Kiki) Janovitz, pp. 24-25; Albert Michini, pp. 26-45; Joel Snyder, pp. 48-72; Howard S. Friedman, p. 73; Pat Stewart, pp. 76-101.

Contents

HAPPENINGS

How do we learn? How do our experiences help us grow? In "Happenings," special things happen to both animals and people. What happens to these characters helps them learn something about themselves and their lives. Some characters grow because of what they learn from others. Some grow because of what happens to them. But all the characters finally realize that the most important thing is to be themselves.

One of the characters you will meet is Wilbur, the pig, who discovers that he cannot be like someone else, but people like him the way he is. You will meet a baby bat and share her adventures. You will meet a boy who has always wanted to fly. You will also meet a boy who tries to protect a special friend.

As you read, think about how the characters in the stories grow. Think about how they change and learn to be themselves. How have your experiences changed you and helped you grow?

Familiar Friends

The horses, the pigs,
And the chickens,
The turkeys, the ducks,
And the sheep!
I can see all my friends
From my window
As soon as I waken
From sleep.

The cat on the fence
Is out walking.
The geese have gone down
For a swim.
The pony comes trotting
Right up to the gate;
He knows I have candy
For him.

The cows in the pasture
Are switching
Their tails to keep off
The flies.
And the old mother dog
Has come out in the yard
With five pups to give me
A surprise.

—*James S. Tippett*

Wilbur's Boast

FROM THE NOVEL,

Charlotte's Web,

BY E. B. WHITE

Charlotte's Web is the story of a pig named Wilbur and his very special friend, the spider Charlotte A. Cavatica.

Wilbur and Charlotte lived with other animals on a farm owned by the Zuckermans. At first, Wilbur didn't like the farm. Lurvy, the farmhand, fed him three times a day. Fern, the young girl who cared for him when he was a weak, little piglet, came to visit every day—if it didn't rain. Still, Wilbur was lonely—until he met Charlotte and found a new friend.

Then an old sheep told Wilbur that one day, when he grew fat, he would be turned into bacon and ham. The news frightened Wilbur. But his friend Charlotte promised to think of a way to save him.

Charlotte did her thinking as she hung from her web, and she weaved on her web every day. One day, however, her work was interrupted by Wilbur's boasting. After that, Charlotte, Fern, and the rat, Templeton, watched a most unusual event.

13

A spider's web is stronger than it looks. Although it is made of thin, delicate strands, the web is not easily broken. However, a web gets torn every day by the insects that kick around in it, and a spider must rebuild it when it gets full of holes. Charlotte liked to do her weaving during the late afternoon, and Fern liked to sit nearby and watch. One afternoon, she heard a most interesting conversation and witnessed a strange event.

"You have awfully hairy legs, Charlotte," said Wilbur, as the spider busily worked at her task.

"My legs are hairy for a good reason," replied Charlotte. "Furthermore, each leg of mine has seven sections—the coxa, the trochanter, the femur, the patella, the tibia, the metatarsus, and the tarsus."

Wilbur sat bolt upright. "You're kidding," he said.

"No, I'm not either."

"Say those names again. I didn't catch them the first time."

"Coxa, trochanter, femur, patella, tibia, metatarsus, and tarsus."

"Goodness!" said Wilbur, looking down at his own chubby legs. "I don't think *my* legs have seven sections."

"Well," said Charlotte, "you and I lead different lives. You don't have to spin a web. That takes real leg work."

"I could spin a web if I tried," said Wilbur, boasting. "I've just never tried."

"Let's see you do it," said Charlotte. Fern chuckled softly, and her eyes grew wide with love for the pig.

"O.K.," replied Wilbur. "You coach me and I'll spin one. It must be a lot of fun to spin a web. How do I start?"

"Take a deep breath!" said Charlotte, smiling. Wilbur breathed deeply. "Now climb to the highest place you can get to, like this." Charlotte raced up to the top of the doorway. Wilbur scrambled to the top of the manure pile.

"Very good!" said Charlotte. "Now make an attachment with your spinnerets, hurl yourself into space, and let out a dragline as you go down!"

Wilbur hesitated a moment, then jumped out into the air. He glanced hastily behind to see if a piece of rope was following him to check his fall. But nothing seemed to be happening in his rear, and the next thing he knew he landed with a thump. "Ooomp!" he grunted.

Charlotte laughed so hard her web began to sway.

"What did I do wrong?" asked the pig, when he recovered from his bump.

"Nothing," said Charlotte. "It was a nice try."

"I think I'll try again," said Wilbur, cheerfully. "I believe what I need is a little piece of string to hold me."

The pig walked out to his yard. "You there, Templeton?" he called. The rat poked his head out from under the trough.

"Got a little piece of string I could borrow?" asked Wilbur. "I need it to spin a web."

"Yes, indeed," replied Templeton, who saved string. "No trouble at all. Anything to oblige." He crept down into his hole, pushed the goose egg out of the way, and

returned with an old piece of dirty, white string. Wilbur examined it.

"That's just the thing," he said. "Tie one end to my tail, will you, Templeton?"

Wilbur crouched low, with his thin, curly tail toward the rat. Templeton seized the string, passed it around the end of the pig's tail, and tied two half hitches. Charlotte watched in delight. Like Fern, she was truly fond of Wilbur, whose smelly pen and stale food attracted the flies she needed, and she was proud to see that he was not a quitter and was willing to try again to spin a web.

While the rat and the spider and the little girl watched, Wilbur climbed again to the top of the manure pile, full of energy and hope.

"Everybody watch!" he cried. Then summoning all his strength, he threw himself into the air, head-first. The string trailed behind him. But as he had neglected to fasten the other end to anything, it didn't do any good, and Wilbur landed with a thud, crushed and hurt. Tears came to his eyes. Templeton grinned. Charlotte just sat quietly. After a bit, she spoke.

"You can't spin a web, Wilbur, and I advise you to put the idea out of your mind. You lack two things needed for spinning a web."

"What are they?" asked Wilbur, sadly.

"You lack a set of spinnerets, and you lack know-how. But cheer up, you don't need a web. Zuckerman supplies you with three big meals a day. Why should you worry about trapping food?"

Wilbur sighed. "You're ever so much cleverer and brighter than I am, Charlotte. I guess I was just trying to show off. Serves me right."

Templeton untied his string and took it back to his home. Charlotte returned to her weaving.

"You needn't feel too badly, Wilbur," she said. "Not many creatures can spin webs. Even men aren't as good at it as spiders, although they *think* they're pretty good, and they'll *try* anything. Did you ever hear of the Queensborough Bridge?"

Wilbur shook his head. "Is it a web?"

"Sort of," replied Charlotte. "But do you know how long it took men to build it? Eight whole years. My goodness, I would have starved to death waiting that long. I can make a web in a single evening."

"What do people catch in the Queensborough Bridge —bugs?" asked Wilbur.

"No," said Charlotte. "They don't catch anything. They just keep trotting back and forth across the bridge thinking there is something better on the other side. If they'd hang head-down at the top of the thing and wait quietly, maybe something good would come along. But no —with men, it's rush, rush, rush, every minute. I'm glad I'm a sedentary spider."

"What does sedentary mean?" asked Wilbur.

"Means I sit still a good part of the time and don't go wandering all over creation. I know a good thing when I see it, and my web is a good thing. I stay put and wait for what comes. Gives me a chance to think."

"Well, I'm sort of sedentary myself, I guess," said the pig. "I have to hang around here whether I want to or not. You know where I'd really like to be this evening?"

"Where?"

"In a forest looking for beechnuts and truffles and delectable roots, pushing leaves aside with my wonderful strong nose, searching and sniffing along the ground, smelling, smelling, smelling . . ."

"You smell just the way you are," remarked a lamb who had just walked in. "I can smell you from here. You're the smelliest creature in the place."

Wilbur hung his head. His eyes grew wet with tears. Charlotte noticed his embarrassment, and she spoke sharply to the lamb.

"Let Wilbur alone!" she said. "He has a perfect right to smell, considering his surroundings. You're no bundle of sweet peas yourself. Furthermore, you are interrupting a very pleasant conversation. What were we talking about, Wilbur, when we were so rudely interrupted?"

"Oh, I don't remember," said Wilbur. "It doesn't make any difference. Let's not talk any more for a while,

Charlotte. I'm getting sleepy. You go ahead and finish fixing your web, and I'll just lie here and watch you. It's a lovely evening." Wilbur stretched out on his side.

Twilight settled over Zuckerman's barn, and a feeling of peace. Fern knew it was almost suppertime, but she couldn't bear to leave. Swallows passed on silent wings, in and out of the doorways, bringing food to their young ones. From across the road, a bird sang, "Whippoorwill, whippoorwill!" Lurvy sat down under an apple tree and lit his pipe; the animals sniffed the familiar smell of strong tobacco. Wilbur heard the trill of the tree toad and the occasional slamming of the kitchen door. All these sounds made him feel comfortable and happy, for he loved life and loved to be a part of the world on a summer evening. But as he lay there, he remembered what the old sheep had told him. The thought of death came to him, and he began to tremble with fear.

"Charlotte?" he said, softly.

"Yes, Wilbur?"

"I don't want to die."

"Of course you don't," said Charlotte, in a comforting voice.

"I just love it here in the barn," said Wilbur. "I love everything about this place."

"Of course you do," said Charlotte. "We all do."

The goose appeared, followed by her seven goslings. They thrust their little necks out and kept up a musical whistling, like a tiny troupe of pipers. Wilbur listened to the sound with love in his heart.

"Charlotte?" he said.

"Yes?" said the spider.

"Were you serious when you promised you would keep them from killing me?"

"I was never more serious in my life. I am not going to let you die, Wilbur."

"How are you going to save me?" asked Wilbur, whose curiosity was very strong on this point.

"Well," said Charlotte, vaguely, "I don't really know. But I'm working on a plan."

"That's wonderful," said Wilbur. "How is the plan coming, Charlotte? Have you got very far with it? Is it coming along pretty well?" Wilbur was trembling again, but Charlotte was cool and collected.

"Oh, it's coming all right," she said, lightly. "The plan is still in its early stages and hasn't completely shaped up yet, but I'm working on it."

"When do you work on it?" begged Wilbur.

"When I'm hanging head-down at the top of my web. That's when I do my thinking, because then all the blood is in my head."

"I'd be only too glad to help in any way I can."

"Oh, I'll work it out alone," said Charlotte. "I can think better if I think alone."

"All right," said Wilbur. "But don't fail to let me know if there's anything I can do to help, no matter how slight."

"Well," replied Charlotte, "you must try to build yourself up. I want you to get plenty of sleep, and stop worrying. Never hurry and never worry! Chew your food thoroughly and eat every bit of it, except you must leave just enough for Templeton. Gain weight and stay well — that's the way you can help. Keep fit, and don't lose your nerve. Do you think you understand?"

"Yes, I understand," said Wilbur.

"Go along to bed, then," said Charlotte. "Sleep is important."

Wilbur trotted over to the darkest corner of his pen and threw himself down. He closed his eyes. In another minute, he spoke.

"Charlotte?" he said.

"Yes, Wilbur?"

"May I go out to my trough and see if I left any of my supper? I think I left just a tiny bit of mashed potato."

"Very well," said Charlotte. "But I want you in bed again without delay."

Wilbur started to race out to his yard.

"Slowly, slowly!" said Charlotte. "Never hurry and never worry!"

Wilbur checked himself and crept slowly to his trough. He found a bit of potato, chewed it carefully, swallowed it, and walked back to bed. He closed his eyes and was silent for a while.

"Charlotte?" he said in a whisper.

"Yes?"

"May I get a drink of milk? I think there are a few drops of milk left in my trough."

"No, the trough is dry, and I want you to go to sleep. No more talking! Close your eyes and go to sleep!"

Wilbur shut his eyes. Fern got up from her stool and started for home, her mind full of everything she had seen and heard.

"Good night, Charlotte!" said Wilbur.

"Good night, Wilbur!"

There was a pause.

"Good night, Charlotte!"

"Good night, Wilbur!"

"Good night!"

"Good night!"

In the days and weeks that followed, Charlotte's plan to save Wilbur gradually took shape. She was growing old, but she was determined to keep her promise to Wilbur. She even persuaded Templeton, the rat, to help her.

Would you like to know Charlotte's plan? Do you think it worked? Why don't you read the novel, Charlotte's Web, to find out?

Feather or Fur

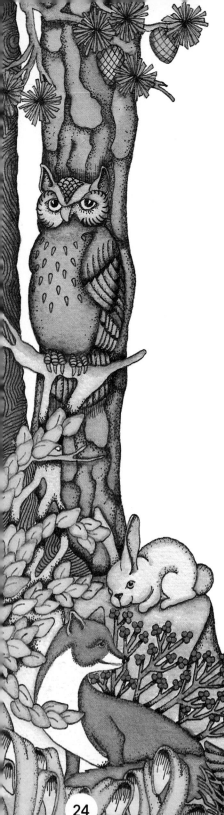

When you watch for
Feather or fur
Feather or fur
Do not stir
Do not stir.

Feather or fur
Come crawling
Creeping
Some come peeping
Some by night
And some by day.
Most come gently
All come softly
Do not scare
A friend away.

When you watch for
Feather or fur
Feather or fur
Do not stir
Do not stir.

—John Becker

Wufu

Berniece Freschet

Part One

Spring

It was a warm rainy night. High in the rafters of an old deserted barn, Wufu, a little brown bat, was born.

The mother bat caught her new baby in her wide wings. She wrapped her wings close about the baby. The tiny, naked, newborn bat snuggled against her mother's warm body and began to nurse.

Wufu's mother hung under the roof in a far corner of the barn, away from a large family of bats. There were sixty-seven members in the bat family. Counting Wufu, now there were sixty-eight. There were uncles, aunts, brothers, sisters, and many, many cousins—all hanging together—upside down—high in the rafters of the old barn.

After a while, the mother bat moved over beside her family. It was cozy here in the darkness. The musty smell of hay drifted up from the hayloft. The little bats all pressed close together for warmth and comfort.

The falling rain made a soft whispering sound against the roof. Soon, when Wufu's stomach was full of milk, she burrowed into her mother's soft fur and slept.

Because of the spring rain, the bats did not leave the barn this night. But the next day, the rain stopped. That evening the bats started out on their usual hunt for food and water.

With a fluttering and flapping of their wide wings, the bats flew out the open door of the hayloft. Three times they circled around the barn. Then, flying high above the treetops, the bats sailed over a wooded hill and swooped down to a small lake.

The darkening air was filled with the sounds of a May twilight. At the edge of the lake, hidden in the reeds, a chorus of toads and frogs croaked a spring concert. From a tree branch above the still water, a hermit thrush answered with its clear, sweet song.

Under a dogwood bush, a marsh hen fluffed out her feathers and settled herself more comfortably over her nest of eggs.

A turtle plunged off a rock and splashed into the lake.

Here and there, a fish leaped up to catch a mosquito, making wide circles of ripples on the water.

Wufu clung tightly to her mother's fur. The mother skimmed low over the lake. She dipped so low that her wing tips almost brushed the surface. She dipped her head down and scooped up a small mouthful of water. She did this several times, flying back and forth, back and forth — each time lapping up a tiny sip of water until her thirst was satisfied.

Suddenly, right in front of her, a fat trout jumped out of the water. His big mouth opened wide. There was no time to move out of his way. Quickly the mother bat dived under the trout. Then, with great energy, she swooped high into the air. She and Wufu had barely missed making a supper for the hungry fish.

The bat family climbed up into the sky and off toward a marshy bog about a mile away. At the bog, the bat family hunted insects to eat. They caught hundreds and hundreds of moths, mosquitoes, and gnats—almost any insect in the air.

The farmer, who lived over the hill, was glad that the bat family had come to live in the old barn. They would catch many of the harmful insects that otherwise would ruin his apple orchard and the new tender plants in his vegetable garden. The bats did the

farmer a great service. He hoped they would stay a long time in the old barn.

As the bats dipped low over the marshy bog, they made a series of high piercing cries. These sounds guided the bats and told them what was ahead of them.

The sounds bounced off any object in their path. With their sensitive ears, the bats could tell from the echo how big the object was and how far away it was. If the object was moving, the echo told them which way it was going. They could even tell the texture of the object. The echoes were different when they came from a stone, a moth, or just a leaf blowing in the wind.

The bats could see in the daytime, but their eyes were small. So at night, they used their ears to "see".

At dawn, the bats flew back to the lake for a last drink of water. Then they headed for their home in the barn.

The sun pushed up over the hill. Its first warm rays inched across the barnyard. They touched the bent and rusty hayfork — then, the smooth round stones in the wall. The rays moved past the old, twisted apple tree and then slowly slanted up the gray, weathered side of the barn—bathing everything in warm, yellow light.

The bat family circled once around the barn and then quickly darted inside the hayloft door. With a great fluttering and flapping of wings, they perched on the rafters. Then, clinging with their long, curved hind toes to the rafters, they swung themselves upside down and huddled together. The mother bat wrapped her wide wings around Wufu.

Here, hanging from the rafters and folded inside their wings, the little brown bats went to sleep in the air.

Every evening, for almost two weeks, the mother bat took her baby with her. But soon Wufu was too heavy to carry. One evening, before the mother bat flew off to hunt for food, she carefully hung Wufu up on a limb of the old apple tree that stood at the side of the barn. All night long, while the bat family looked for insects to eat, Wufu would stay there. She was well-hidden among the leaves and the sweet-smelling apple blossoms in the tree.

The moon came up. A dark shadow skimmed overhead. Silently, the shadow swooped through the hayloft door. It was a barn owl — a dangerous enemy. He was looking for something to eat — a small bat would be a tempting morsel for his supper. Finding nothing in the barn, the owl flew outside and perched at the top of the apple tree.

He flapped his wings and snapped his sharp beak.

His head turned slowly from side to side.

His round yellow eyes looked out. His sight was very sharp. He could see the black beetle that stirred the grasses below.

The hungry owl watched and waited.

Wufu hung silently on the limb. Her small, dark body blended into the shadow of leaves. The little bat slept soundly. She did not know that an enemy was near. A soft wind ruffled the leaves. It gently rocked Wufu back and forth on her limb. In the darkness, she looked like just another leaf swaying in the breeze.

Below, beside the stone wall, a meadow mouse poked her head out of a hole.

The owl blinked. His eyes stared down into the darkness.

The mouse pushed outside and sat up on her hind legs. She looked around — sniffing the air for signs of danger. Then, quickly, she scurried up the wall and ran over the top of the smooth stones.

The owl leaped far out. The quiet hunter dived low. His sharp claws spread wide.

The owl's shadow passed over the mouse. Squeaking with fright, the mouse jumped — flattening herself into a crack between the stones.

Tonight the mouse and the little brown bat were lucky. They had escaped the quiet hunter.

The barn owl pulled in his claws, dipped his wings, and swooped upward. From out of the darkness came his cry as he silently glided away: "Whoo — whoo — whoo — "

During the day, when the other bats were sleeping, sometimes Wufu would awake. Gradually, she became aware that there were other creatures who lived below her in the barn.

Inside an old, worn horse collar that hung from a peg on the barn wall, lived a family of field mice. The mouse babies were still too young to leave the nest. Sometimes, when their mother was away looking for food, the young mice poked their heads out of a hole in the collar. Five pairs of black, shiny eyes looked out. Five tiny noses twitched. What a big world waited outside their home!

One day, a black snake crawled into the barn. Slowly, she slithered forward. Her scales made a soft rustling sound against the dry dirt floor.

The young mice watched the black snake wriggling nearer. The snake's tongue flicked in and out, in and out, testing the air for scent of prey. The snake smelled mouse. She raised her body high.

But the wise mother mouse had chosen a good place to have her family. The black snake could not reach the baby mice in the horse collar on the wall.

Finally, the snake turned and slowly crawled out of the barn. But she would be back.

High above, Wufu clung tightly to her mother's fur. If she were to fall, the black snake would enjoy a breakfast of bat almost as much as one of mouse.

On the other side of the barn, underneath the corncrib, lived a skunk. Most of the time, she slept during the day and, like the bat family, hunted for her food at night. But sometimes, she came out in the daytime and shuffled about the barn, sniffing into the dark corners looking for insects to eat.

One morning, three baby skunks followed her out of the corncrib. From above, Wufu watched the skunk family.

At first, the babies stayed close to the crib. When they walked, they staggered about and bumped into each other. But gradually, their legs grew strong. Soon they were playing together. They began to stray farther and farther from the safety of their home.

But whenever a baby skunk wandered too far, the mother skunk went after it. Holding it in her mouth by the scruff of its neck, she carried it back to the safety of the corncrib.

One evening, as the bats fluttered out of the hayloft, the mother skunk was leading her babies out the door. It was time for the youngsters to learn how to find their own food.

While the bats hunted in the sky, the mother skunk was teaching her young to hunt on the ground. They learned to poke under logs and rocks for grubs and beetles. They found the place where the snapping turtle had laid her eggs on the shore of the lake. They learned how to use their quick paws to bat minnows out of the water.

At dawn, the bat family came swooping back into the hayloft.

At the same time, the mother skunk was leading her weary youngsters into the barn, back to the corncrib for a long, well-earned day's rest.

It had been a busy night for the little skunks. They were very tired. They curled up into furry balls and were soon asleep.

Hanging from their rafters above, the sleepy cluster of bats snuggled together. The old barn grew quiet.

Part Two

Summer, Autumn, Winter

Small green knobs began to form on the branches of the apple tree.

Wufu was growing. She was three and a half weeks old now and almost four inches long. For several nights, she had taken short practice flights out from her limb on the apple tree. She was beginning to get the feel of flying through the air. She was learning how to use her remarkable wings.

Wufu's wings were leathery membranes. They stretched between the long bones of her four fingers like a web. The wings stretched from her shoulders to her hind feet and back to her tail. A membrane was attached to all four legs and to her tail. It made a kind of parachute above her body as she flew. These wings made the little brown bat one of the most skillful fliers in the sky. But on the ground, Wufu was almost totally helpless.

Her hind legs were smaller than her forearms. Because her knee joints bent backward, it was difficult for her to walk. She moved by pushing her wings against the ground, awkwardly hitching herself forward.

If an enemy were to catch Wufu on the ground, it would be very dangerous for the little bat.

Moonlight shone through the open spaces of the apple tree. It made lacy leaf shadows on the ground. Wufu fluttered out from her branch. She circled the tree and then darted back to her favorite limb.

Above, the owl sat at the top of the tree. His round yellow eyes watched the bat's every move. On her next practice flight from the tree, just as Wufu was fluttering back to her branch — the barn owl sprung outward.

He dived at the little bat!

Wufu did not see the owl, but her sensitive ears heard the vibrations of even this great soft flier. The bat swooped upward.

Quickly, the barn owl followed. But the bat's leathery wings had grown strong. The owl was no match in the sky for the speed of the little brown bat.

Away Wufu sailed — over the treetops — over the hill — skimming across the lake, and then darting down to join her family at the bog.

Soon she, too, was catching the moths and gnats that flitted through the darkness.

No one had to teach her to catch insects. She knew by instinct. She curled her tail forward, making a net that scooped the insects out of the air.

Bending her head forward, she grasped the insects in her mouth. Wufu caught and ate hundreds and hundreds of gnats and moths. She ate almost a fourth of her own weight during just this one night's hunt.

Wufu would have to do this every night of her life. Now she was on her own. She was a hunter. She swooped through the air — a true member of the bat family.

High above, the stars made silver pinpoints of light in a black velvet sky. The moon shone down on the bog. The warm summer night was filled with the soft sounds and quiet movements of the night creatures.

Below, two raccoons sat dipping their paws into the water looking for snails and crayfish to eat. A mother possum, her babies clinging to her back, slowly felt her way down the river's bank. The possums pushed through clumps of rose-colored wild geraniums. The possums had come to the bog for their evening drink and to look for root bulbs to eat.

Under lacy ferns, crickets chirruped. At the swampy edge of the bog, among tall stalks of cattails, frogs sang. The sounds of night were all about.

A curlew and a plover probed in the mud with their long beaks. The two birds hunted for worms and chatted together softly.

A porcupine shuffled over the ground, rustling through the wild grasses.

High above, the little brown bats flitted through the air hunting for insects. In the light of the bright moon, the black shadow of their wings could be seen. The bats flew in graceful, gliding waves under the starry sky.

All night long, on wide, silent wings, they swooped and soared. They looped and whirled — up and down — around and around. The little bats danced through the air, performing a beautiful ballet across the sky.

In the east, the horizon grew light. The moon slid behind the hill. One by one, the bright stars grew dim. It was time for the bats to return to their home in the barn. Back they flew.

Clinging to her rafter in the barn, Wufu began to wash herself. The little brown bat liked to keep clean, and sometimes she spent an hour grooming herself. Like a cat, Wufu licked the glossy brown fur on her back and then the lighter fur across her stomach. She moistened the tip of one wing and rubbed it hard across her head, against the fur.

Then, very carefully, Wufu cleaned her ears. Her ears were a matter of life and death to the little bat. So she gave them special care. Licking her thumb, she twisted it around and around in her ear until she was satisfied that it was washed thoroughly clean. Then she scratched behind it.

She also paid particular attention to her wings. She sponged every inch with her long red tongue. Working on the inside, she pulled the wing down over her head. The elastic membrane stretched into odd-looking shapes. The little bat looked as though she were wearing a rubber mask. Finally, she was satisfied with herself.

Wufu's face wrinkled into a wide yawn. She stretched. She was tired from her first long, all-night flight. Soon she dozed. Later she half awoke and snuggled over closer beside her mother. Suddenly — a piece of rotting wood gave way. Wufu lost her grip on the rafter. She plunged downward!

She had barely enough time to half spread her wings and break the fall before she hit the ground.

The fall stunned her. She closed her eyes and huddled against the floor. She was afraid and didn't know what to do.

She heard a soft rustling sound moving near. A blurred shadow crawled through the barn doorway and slowly moved toward the bat on the ground.

The big black snake raised her head. Her flicking tongue caught the bat's scent. She weaved forward.

Wufu struggled to her feet. She knew she was in serious danger. It was hard for her to move across the floor. But the confused little bat tried hard to get away from the enemy.

Slowly, softly the snake slithered nearer. She raised her head and pulled it back, ready to strike —

Wufu spread her wings. With her last bit of strength, she lifted herself upward. Then she was in the air — flying! But she did not have enough strength to reach the rafters high above. Suddenly, her wings folded and hung limp. Wufu was falling again.

She flung out her feet behind her. Her long toenails dug into the horse-collar peg. She clung there. For a moment, she was safe.

A mouse peeked out of her hole in the horse-collar. With angry squeaks, she scolded the bat for disturbing her sleep.

Wufu rested. She waited for her strength to return. She paid little attention to the angry mouse.

The bat and the mouse looked as though they might be cousins. With her pug nose and her small black eyes almost hidden in the folds of her wrinkled skin, Wufu looked very much like a furry mouse with wings.

The hungry snake grew tired of waiting for the bat to fall. She crawled away, out the barn door.

The apples on the old twisted tree grew round and red.

All summer long, the bats hunted at the bog. They returned early each morning to sleep away the hot summer days under the roof of the cool, dark barn.

For weeks they had been eating and eating, and they had grown fat. Each day, the bats moved a little slower and slept longer. Now it was almost time for the bat family to go into hibernation, to move into their cave up in the hills. There they would sleep through the long winter.

The autumn nights grew crisp and cold.

Ripe apples fell from the apple tree.

A hungry family of deer came and ate the fruit.

The pumpkins in the farmer's garden grew round and golden.

One twilight evening the bats swooped away — over the treetops — over the hills. Their wide scalloped wings made a beautiful black pattern against the red sunset. This time, they would not return to the barn at dawn.

The farmer watched them go. His harvest had been good. He was grateful for the little brown bats' help. He would be glad when they returned in the spring.

Snows drifted deep against the stone wall and the gray weathered sides of the barn. Cold winds whistled through the bare branches of the apple tree.

In the hills, deep underground in their warm cave, the bats slept — snuggled close. All through the long winter, the bats would sleep their deep sleep.

When the warm breezes of spring come and melt the snow, and the sap once again rises in the apple tree and tiny green buds push out, the brown bats will return.

Then Wufu and the bat family will stay, high in the rafters under the roof of the old, deserted barn — their home.

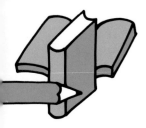

Getting to Know You

Reading a story is like moving to a new town. When you read, you have a chance to explore a new place and meet new friends. The people you meet in a story are the *characters*. You learn about them from the things they think, do, and say. You also learn about them from the way they behave toward other characters.

You learned many things about Charlotte, the spider, in "Wilbur's Boast." For example, Charlotte liked Wilbur, the pig, and was a good friend to him. You learned how she felt about Wilbur from the way she acted and spoke. She enjoyed talking to Wilbur. When he wanted to spin a web, she showed him how and encouraged him. When he realized he couldn't, she consoled him. She explained things to Wilbur that he didn't understand. She came to Wilbur's defense and spoke sharply to the lamb who insulted him. Charlotte also comforted Wilbur by telling him she was working on a plan to save him.

You learned about Wilbur, too, from the things he said, thought, and did. You learned that he could be very determined and wouldn't give up when he made up his mind. For example, he tried twice to spin a web. Then, when he told Charlotte how smart she was, you learned that he looked up to her.

Read the story below. As you read, pay close attention to the character named Tommy.

Tommy was a lazy young man. He never did his work until the last minute. His friends often teased him. "Some day you'll be sorry," they warned. But Tommy just laughed at their warnings.

In school, the teacher gave the students three weeks in which to prepare a report. The other students went to the library immediately. But Tommy didn't go.

"I'll do my work on the last day," he thought. But on the last day, it snowed heavily. Tommy couldn't get to the library. The next day, he told his teacher what had happened. Some children laughed to themselves. Others laughed aloud.

Tommy thought, "I'm really ashamed of myself." Then he said aloud, "I've learned my lesson."

Tommy was never late again.

Now write a sentence from the story that proves each statement below:

1. Tommy's own thoughts showed that he was lazy.
2. Tommy's own actions showed that he was lazy.
3. Other people's actions showed that Tommy was not respected.
4. Tommy's own thoughts showed that he was sorry.
5. Tommy's own words told you he was sorry.
6. Tommy's own actions showed that he was truly sorry.

HAWK, I'm Your Brother

Byrd Baylor

Rudy Soto
dreams
of flying . . .

wants
to float
on the wind,
wants
to soar
over canyons.

He doesn't see himself
some little
light-winged bird
that flaps
and flutters
when it flies.
No cactus wren.
No sparrow.

He'd be
more like
a HAWK

gliding

smoother
than anything else
in the world.

He sees himself
a hawk
wrapped up in wind

lifting

facing the sun.

That's how
he wants
to fly.

That's all
he wants—
the only wish
he's ever had.

No matter what happens
he won't give it up.
He won't trade it
for easier wishes.

There,
playing alone
on the mountainside,
a dark skinny boy
calling out
to a hawk . . .

That's Rudy Soto.

People here say
that the day he was born
he looked at the sky
and lifted his hands
toward birds
and seemed to smile
at Santos Mountain.

The first words
he ever learned
were the words for
FLYING
and for
BIRD
and for
UP THERE . . . UP THERE.

And later on
they say that
every day
he asked his father,
"When do I learn to fly?"

(He was too young then
to know
he'd never get his wish.)

His father said,
"You run.
You climb over rocks.
You jump around like a crazy
whirlwind.
Why do you need to fly?"

"I just do.
I need to fly."

In those days
he thought that
somebody
would give him
the answer.
He asked
everybody . . .

everybody.

And they always said,
"People don't fly."

"Never?"

"Never."

But Rudy Soto
told them this:
"*Some* people do.
Maybe we just don't know
those people.
Maybe they live
far away from here."

And when he met new people
he would
look at them
carefully.

"Can you fly?"

They'd only laugh
and shake their heads.

Finally he learned
to stop
asking.

Still
he thought
that maybe
flying
is the secret
old people
keep
to themselves.
Maybe they go sailing
quietly
through the sky
when children
are asleep.

Or maybe
flying
is for
magic people.

And he even thought
that if no one else
in the world
could fly
he'd be the one
who would learn it.

"Somebody ought to,"
he said.
"Somebody.
Me!
Rudy Soto."

There,
barefoot
on the mountainside,
he'd
almost
fly.

He'd dream
he knew
the power
of great wings
and sing
up to the sun.

In his mind
he always seemed
to be a hawk,
the way he flew.

Of course
a boy like that
would know
every nest
this side of the mountain.
He'd know the time
in summer
when the young hawks
learn to fly.
And he'd think
a thousand times,
"Hawk, I'm your
brother.
Why am I stuck
down here?"

You have to know all this
to forgive the boy
for what he did.

And even then
you may not think
that he was right
to steal the bird.
It may seem
cruel
and selfish
and mean—
not worthy of one
who says
he's brother
to all birds.

But anyway
that's what he did.

He stole
a hawk—
a redtail hawk—
out of its nest
before the bird
could fly.

It was a nest
that Rudy Soto
must have seen
all his life,
high on the ledge
of a steep rough
canyon wall.

He thought
that nest
might be
the best home
in the world,
up there
on Santos Mountain.

And he even thought
that there might be
some special
magic
in a bird
that came from
Santos Mountain.

Somehow
he thought
he'd share
that
magic

and he'd *fly*.

They say
it used to
be
that way
when
we
knew how
to
talk
to birds

and how
to call
a bird's
wild spirit
down
into our own.

He'd heard
all those
old stories

and he'd seen
hawks
go flying
over mountains
and felt
their power
fill the sky.

It seemed to him
he'd FLY —

if
a hawk
became
his
brother.

That's why
he climbed
the cliff
at dawn
singing . . .

to make
the magic
stronger.

And
that's why
he left
an offering
of food . . .

to show
he was
that
brother.

But
the young hawk
struggled
and screamed,
called
to the birds
circling
overhead,
called
to its nest
on Santos Mountain.

"Listen, bird.
Don't be afraid.
Don't be
afraid
of me."

Climbing down,
he held
that bird
so close
he felt
its heartbeat
and
the bird
felt his.

"You'll be
all right.
You'll see."

But even a hawk
too young to fly
knows
he's meant
to fly.
He knows
he isn't meant
to have
a string
tied
to his leg.

He knows
he isn't meant
to live
in a cage.

Every day
he screams.
He pulls
against the string.
He beats
his wings
against the cage.

"You'll be happy
with me, bird.
You will."

But the bird
looks out
with fierce
free
eyes
and calls
to its brothers
in the canyon.

Every day
it is the same.

They see
those
other birds
learning
to fly,
learning
the touch
and roll
and lift
of air,
learning
to
dip
and dive.
They turn
when
the wind
turns.

But
down below
with his feet
touching
sand
Rudy Soto's hawk
can only
flap
his wings
and rise
as high
as a string
will let him go.

Not high
enough.

Not far
enough.

Rudy Soto
tells his hawk:
"Someday
we'll fly
together."

He wants
to please
that hawk.
He's sure
he will.
He's sure
it's going to be
his
brother.

Each day
when the melons
are picked
and the wood
is chopped
and the corn
is hoed
Rudy Soto gives
a long soft call
and he comes
running.

He always says:
"I'm here now,
bird.
What do you want
to do?"

He takes the bird
out of the cage
and ties the string
around its foot
and the bird sits
on his shoulder
as they walk
the desert hills.

They go down
sandy washes
and
follow
deer tracks
into canyons.

Sometimes
they sit
looking off
to
Santos Mountain.

And sometimes
they even go
on the other side
of Santos Mountain
to a place
where
water
trickles
over
flat
smooth
rocks.

The bird
plays
in that
cold water . . .
dips
his wings
into the stream
and jumps
and flaps

and the boy says,
"See.
You're happy
here with me."

But
even
when he says it
he knows
it isn't true
because
the bird
is tugging
at the string

and
you see
sky
reflected in his eyes

and his eyes
flash

and his wings
move
with the
wind.

You can tell
he
wants
to
fly.

You can tell
that's
all
he wants,
the only
dream
he has.

Rudy Soto
knows
what
it is like
to want
to
fly.

He knows
himself
what
it is like
to have
a dream.

But even so
he waits
until
the end of summer,
hoping
that
the bird
will be
content.

Every day
it is the same.

The bird
still
tugs
and pulls
and yearns
against the string.

Rudy Soto
knows
that the hawk
will not
give up.

What else
can
a boy
like Rudy Soto
do?

He has to say:
"I don't want
to see you
so unhappy,
bird."

And he has to say:
"One of us
might as well
fly!"

What else
can he
do
if he
really
loves
that bird?

He has to
take him
back
to Santos Mountain
to the place
where *he*
would like
to fly.

That's where
they go —

up
to those
high
red rocks.

There is
a wind
and
clouds move
across
the sky
and
from far away
you can smell
rain.

Now he
unties
the string
that has held
his hawk
so
long.

The hawk
is on his
shoulder.

"Fly now,
bird.
Go on."

The hawk
turns.
He moves
his wings.

"Bird,
you can
fly."

The hawk
takes
his
time.

There
on the rocks
he jumps
and
flaps,

rises

and
sinks.

He
has
to learn
the force
of air
and the pull
of wind
and the feel
of
freedom.

Maybe
he jumps
a hundred times
before
he seems
to catch
the wind,
before
he lifts
himself
into
that
summer sky.

At last
he
soars.

His wings
shine
in the sun

and
the way
he
flies
is the way
Rudy Soto
always
dreamed
he'd fly.

The bird
looks
down.

Then
he calls
a long
hawk cry,
the kind of cry
he used to call
to his
brothers.

Brother
to
brother
they call

all through
the afternoon.

Only
this time
he calls
to
Rudy Soto

High
on the side
of Santos Mountain
Rudy Soto
lifts
his arms.

and the sound
floats
on the wind.

Rudy Soto
answers
with
the same
hawk
sound.

His hair
blows
in the wind
and
in his mind

he's
FLYING
too.

Back and forth
they call.

It doesn't
even matter
that
his feet
are on the
ground.

It seems to him
he has
the whole sky
to fly in
when
he hears
that
call.

He knows
he'll keep it
in his mind
forever.

Rudy Soto
doesn't tell
anybody.

He doesn't say:
"Lucky me.
I know
about
flying.
I know
about
wind."

He never says,
"There is a hawk
that is
my brother
so I have
a special
power."

71

But
people here
can tell
such things.

They notice
that a hawk
calls to him
from
Santos Mountain

and they hear
the way
he answers.

They see
that Rudy Soto
has a
different look
about him.

His eyes
flash
like
a young
hawk's
eyes

and there is
sky
reflected

in those eyes
and it's
the sky
high
over
Santos Mountain.

People here
are not
surprised.

They're
wise enough
to
understand
such things.

Hurt No Living Thing

Hurt no living thing;
Ladybird, nor butterfly,
Nor moth with dusty wing.
Nor cricket chirping cheerily,
Nor grasshopper so light of leap,
Nor dancing gnat, nor beetle fat,
Nor harmless worms that creep.

–Christina Rossetti

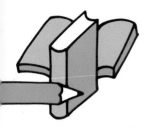

Categories and Labels

Ruth runs a department store. She sells furniture, books, and toys. All the books are on the first floor. All the furniture is on the second floor. The third floor has all the toys.

Bill runs a department store, too. He also sells furniture, books, and toys. However, these items are scattered throughout the store. Some books are on the first floor. Others are on the second and third floors. The same is true of the furniture and the toys.

Suppose you wanted to buy a dictionary. Would you rather shop at Ruth's store or Bill's store? You would save time at Ruth's store. She has grouped all her books together. Bill's dictionaries might be on any one of three floors.

Putting things into groups is called *classifying*. You put things that are alike in the same group. For example, one group of things in a store might be books. The items in that group may be a dictionary, a cookbook, a biography, and an almanac. Here are other groups and some items that might be in these groups.

Group	Items
Furniture:	chair, table, bed, lamp
Toys:	yo-yo, rubber ball, top, blocks

ACTIVITY A   Read each set of items. Then read the group names. Choose the correct group name for each set of items. Write the group name on your paper.

1. **Items:** mouse, horse, dog, monkey, squirrel
   Group: colors, animals, shoes
2. **Items:** bread, eggs, cheese, meat, tomatoes
   Group: foods, jobs, countries
3. **Items:** three, six, twelve, nine, twenty
   Group: names of rivers, names of towns, names of numbers

ACTIVITY B   Read each set of words. One word in each set names the group. On your paper, write the word that names the group.

1. milk, juice, cream, liquids, water, soda
2. big, small, medium, large, sizes, tiny
3. snow, weather, rain, sunshine, fog, sleet
4. glass, steel, rubber, cotton, wool, materials
5. golf, tennis, sports, baseball, soccer, basketball

ACTIVITY C   Read each set of words. Think of a group name for each set. Write the group name on your paper.

1. January, April, July, November, December
2. shirt, pants, socks, sweater, skirt
3. yellow, white, blue, pink, green
4. river, lake, stream, pond, creek
5. Tuesday, Friday, Thursday, Sunday, Wednesday

MY CARUSO

Earl G. Robbins

PART ONE
I MEET CARUSO

The train slowed, tooted its whistle three times, and came to a full stop in front of the little depot. The kindly conductor, who had looked after me since leaving the city one hundred miles away, collected my ticket and helped me onto the platform. I spied Grandpa on his wagon, holding the mules and making ready to drive us to the farm. "Here I am, Grandpa. Here I am!" I cried, running and climbing on the high seat beside him. "This summer is mine, Grandpa. This summer is mine!" And that summer was mine. No other grandchildren lived within miles, and the nearest neighbors were an hour's wagon ride away.

The very first afternoon, Grandpa and I walked down a hill to a cool pool of water under the railroad trestle. First we swam. I played and paddled in shallow water near the bank. Grandpa swam like a frog. His arms and legs worked sidewise from his body, rather than forward and back, as most people swim. He dove and ducked me playfully. Later we fished. We caught small fish, but threw them back into the stream to grow.

Grandpa joked like a young man, not like one who was seventy years old. He mimicked birds, croaked like frogs, and sang funny songs about varmints we saw in the fields and woods. His clear voice rang from hill to hill when he bellowed:

"'Coon has got a ringey tail,
Possum tail go bare.
Rabbit got no tail at all.
Just a little white bunch of hair."

After Sunday dinner, Grandpa and Uncle George sat in the yard and talked about the weather and their crops. I played with Old Jack, Grandpa's furry dog. I chased him and threw him to the ground. Grandpa laughed and joked with me.

Uncle George talked sadly and looked glum. "The weeds are ruining my corn, Pa. I have no one to help me, now that Fanny's gone," he said sadly.

Late in the afternoon as he was preparing to leave, he called me over to where he sat. "Boy," he said, looking me over sharply. "I might use you a few days if you could drive a team of mules." He moved out of his chair as if to leave. "I doubt if you could handle the job," he said, not quite believing his own judgment.

I threw back my shoulders and stood before him. "Uncle George, I can drive your mules. I'm nine years old, going on ten!" I looked up into his weak gray eyes. Then I turned to Grandpa. "Can't I drive the team, Grandpa?"

"The boy's a good hand with my team, George. We plowed weeds out of the watermelons."

"I'll pay you a quarter a day, son, if you can drive Beck and Julie." Uncle George reached into his pocket and pulled out two shiny quarters.

My eyes grew large. "I'm ready, Uncle George. Let's get started."

"Can we have him back by Wednesday, George? I need him to help me drive the mules to town," said Grandpa.

I bubbled with this attention.

"It depends on how good he is with the team, Pa. I usually plow both fields in two and a half days." Uncle George looked at me questioningly. "It might take three days with him."

I was angry. "I'll show you, Uncle George! Heck, I make Grandpa's big mules gallop. I can drive little Beck and Julie!"

A pale moon lit the sky dimly as Uncle George and I walked slowly along a narrow path through the woods leading to his home. The night was dark and quiet when we reached Uncle George's cabin. "We'll be out early, son," he said, striking a match and lighting the lamp. "I want to be in the field by sunup."

As we ate, we talked. "Will we do anything besides plow corn?" I asked. I was thinking of fishing and swimming as I did with Grandpa.

"That's all, except feed the chickens and milk the cow." Uncle George backed his chair away from the table. "Let's go outside and look at the moon before

we go to bed." He moved toward the door. I followed close behind.

Fluffy gray clouds floated slowly across the silent sky. Silhouettes from the pale moon slithered
through a dying, half-naked tree beside the cabin.
Uncle George's thin frame cast a giant shadow away
from his body. A barn owl called softly, "Who, who,
who, who are you?" I felt it was talking to me. It
gave me an eerie feeling. I shivered and wondered if
I had done the right thing in accepting Uncle
George's invitation. A strange loneliness in him
made me homesick. I wished for Old Jack. He
would bark and scare bad things away.

"Let's go to bed so we can be out early," Uncle
George finally said. I crawled into bed and slid to
the backside near the wall. I pulled the cover high
over my head and shut my eyes tightly.

It was yet dark when I was awakened by a voice
saying, "Get up, boy, it's time to feed and milk." I
jumped out of bed and pulled on my overalls. We
had slept soundly, or at least I had, all night long.

Uncle George grinned and pulled on his heavy
shoes. "We'll feed the chickens on the way to the
barn. Take this basket and get some corn from the
bin. I'll start the fire and put my coffee on before we
leave."

I scooped corn into the basket and handed him
a few sticks of wood to put into the stove. He
picked up the milk pail from a bench beside the

door. I walked closely beside him toward the barn. Moist morning air made me feel fresh and clean. Chickens gathered around Uncle George's feet as he stepped through the gate. They clucked, begged, and pecked for favored feeding positions. One rooster, however, did not come close and did not show interest in the plump, yellow grains we scattered over the hungry mob. He stood off and watched like a guard.

Even in the early light, I saw that this rooster was different from the others. His bright feathers and the way he walked gave him a look of royalty. I hoped to see him in full light when we returned.

I did! As we came toward the cabin, he strutted out before us. He threw his head high and gave a clear shrill, "Cock-a-doodle-doo-o." I watched him flap his colorful wings and fly to the top of a post. He arched his shining neck, looked at me, and repeated his "Cock-a-doodle-doo-o." He flew down from his perch and was surrounded by the hens. Other roosters watched with jealousy. He talked, cooed, and moved masterfully among the hens. He strutted, looked toward the less-attractive roosters, and gave another "Cock-a-doodle-doo-o."

A full-grown pullet with a bright red comb moved coyly near the handsome rooster. She fluffed her pretty feathers and clucked softly. He yanked and tore at a clump of heavy sod; uncovered a plump, white grub; and cooed gently to the pretty pullet, calling her to come see what he had. He fanned dirt from around the grub, picked it up graciously, and laid it at the feet of the enchanted young hen.

I watched excitedly as he continued his courtship and wooing. He carried himself with the air of a king. Like the pullet, I too fell in love with him. He strutted and pranced, displaying his bright colors in the early morning light. He was red, green, gold, and deep violet — a rainbow of colors! His full red comb sat above his shapely head like a king's hunting cap. Beneath his strong, curved beak, silver-white wattles swung and flapped like beads of precious pearls decorating his broad breast. His razor-sharp spurs and long claws gave him a fierce bearing. He acted and looked like a conqueror. I knew I must own him.

At breakfast, I asked Uncle George how much he would take for the handsome rooster. He gulped, held his fork in mid-air, stared at me as if unsure of my question, laid his fork on the table, saucered his coffee, and looked at the bed where Aunt Fanny had lain. Finally, he said in a sad voice, "We never thought of selling *that* rooster, son. Fanny named him just before she died. 'My Caruso' she called him, after that big singer that she once heard on a gramophone machine. He crowed and sang at her window every morning at break of day. She said that rooster's 'Cock-a-doodle-doo-o' was like sweet music to her ears." He drank slowly and seemed to forget that I was in the cabin.

I sensed Uncle George might not part with the rooster, but he seemed to be thinking as he buttered a biscuit and covered it with honey. After a long silence, he stared at me and said, "Son, I've been thinking about what Fanny would want me to do." He looked again at her bed. "If you work real hard and we plow both fields by tomorrow night, I might sell Caruso to you for fifty cents." He cleared his throat with a sip of coffee. "I think Fanny would like for a boy like you to own her Caruso."

"I'm ready to work right now, Uncle George! Let's get started. I'll work hard for you." I squirmed and fretted at Uncle George's tardiness. I gobbled down my breakfast. "Let's get started, Uncle George," I said again. "The mules have eaten their corn by this time. Let's go!" With that, I ran to the barn, and Uncle George followed me.

"You don't have to worry about Caruso's feed, boy. He eats worms, bugs, seeds, and wild berries." Uncle George finished hitching Julie to her whiffletree. "We'll plow the rough hillside field first while you and the mules are fresh." He handed me the lines and called out gently, "Get up, Beck. Come on, Julie. Get up Beck. Come on, Julie."

Soon we were in the tall corn. My job was to guide the mules, keeping them at the proper pace and making sure they didn't tramp on the growing corn. I sat on a sack of straw directly behind the mules. Uncle George walked behind, controlling the plow shovels as they scratched and dug out weeds. He talked kindly to the mules, never raising his voice except when the plow snagged into a wild root or a rock. Then, he hollered, "Whoa! Back, Beck. Back up, Julie! Whoa! Whoa, girl!" He shook the plow handles fiercely. Up and down, up and down, he thrashed at weeds and trash until the plow was free and clean.

I clucked and called loudly to the mules. I shook their lines and encouraged them to walk fast. They walked briskly in the morning coolness, wiggling their long ears and switching their stubby tails. The sharp shovels cut and threw dirt high. I hollered, "Get up Julie!" I tapped her sharply with the line. She jumped and broke into a hopping canter, up and down, up and down. Beck stomped, knocked down corn, and kicked against the plow. Sparks flew into my face. I pulled and yanked hard on the lines. Beck and Julie ran zigzagging between the corn rows.

Uncle George socked the plow shovels deep into the ground. "Hold 'em, boy! Hold 'em! Pull 'em back! Hold 'em down! They're running away!" he hollered. He braced his feet and tried to stop the plow.

I seesawed on the lines. I yanked and pulled. "Whoa, Beck! Whoa, Julie! Whoa! Whoa! Whoa, girls!" I pleaded. Over and over, I hollered, "Whoa! Whoa! Whoa! Beck! Whoa! Julie!" The mules only ran faster. Dirt flew. The plow rocked and rolled under me. I wrapped my legs around the frame of the plow to keep from falling and being sheared by the sharp shovels.

Uncle George dragged along behind, panting, pleading, and screaming, "Whoa! Whoa! Whoa! Hold 'em, boy! Hold 'em!" Tall corn slapped and beat his face. Julie and Beck flew to the end of the row. There they stopped and picked grass quietly by the fence.

Uncle George walked around the plow and came up to me. He frowned and mumbled under his breath. He grabbed my arm and held it tightly. My arm ached. "Son," he said angrily, "maybe you can beat and punch Pa's old stacks-of-bones, but don't you ever lay a line on my mules again!" He pinched my arm hard. "I'll send you home this minute!" His hot breath hit my face. "Now, run back down that row and get my hat. I've a mind to send you home right now!"

I jumped off the plow and started after his hat. "Wait!" he commanded sternly. "Do you think you can drive like I tell you to?" He pulled off a shoe and shook dirt out of it.

"I—I—I'll try, Uncle George," I said trembling. "I—I'll try. I'm sorry." I sniffled as I ran for his hat. I was sure I had lost the beautiful rooster.

"Now, do you think you can drive them right, boy?" he asked as I handed him his tattered, dusty hat. He said this in his calm, slow voice.

"I'll try my best, Uncle George. Honest I will. I'll try."

"Talk mule talk to Beck and Julie like I do, easy and low."

 I pulled on the lines easy-like and spoke softly, "Get up, Beck. Come on, Julie," I said quietly. They walked slowly, pulling the plow back and forth, back and forth across the field. Uncle George smiled. He concentrated on getting out all the weeds.

"Gee. Haw. Whoa. Back. Get up," I said quietly. I pulled the lines lightly. Beck and Julie understood and minded me. My work grew easy. I daydreamed. I wondered what to do with my Caruso, as I now thought him to be. "Shall I take him home to the city or leave him with Grandma's chickens?" I asked myself. I hummed and whistled tunes that I had learned in school. I watched the birds fly down from trees, grab worms, and fly away with the worms wiggling and squirming.

I did everything Uncle George asked. I ran for the cow and drove her in at milking time, fed the chickens, split kindling, and straightened covers on the beds. I would have worked through dinner and supper, too, to own Caruso. "It isn't dark yet," I pleaded when we finished plowing the hillside field.

"Let's start the flat field and plow some more before supper."

"No, son, the mules are tired, and so am I." He stopped and rested on a tree stump beside the path. "We've done enough for one day." He pointed to dark cloud banks. "If those clouds don't stir up a storm, we might finish by sundown tomorrow."

"A rain, Uncle George?" I asked in a worried voice. I feared I would not get Caruso if it rained.

"Maybe and maybe not," he said.

Late Tuesday evening, we plowed the last row of the flat field. "Caruso is mine, Uncle George. Caruso is mine." I called. I laughed and hollered, "Caruso is mine! Caruso is mine!" I said over and over.

"You earned him fair and square, son," he replied in a lifeless voice.

PART TWO
CARUSO AND ME

I hurried Beck and Julie toward the barn, where Uncle George and I unharnessed them. Then I rushed the mules into a pasture. Finally, I rushed Uncle George into the chicken shed. He talked quietly, "Here, Caruso. Here, boy. Come to me, Caruso," he coaxed. Caruso moved cautiously to a far corner. He watched with a startled look in his eye. Uncle George stooped low, on a level with Caruso, and grabbed him by both legs. Caruso squawked, "Awe! Awe! Awe!" He flapped and beat Uncle George's arms with his wings. "Awe! Awe! Awe!" he cried, fighting to free himself.

"Watch him fight! This is a strong rooster, boy!" Uncle George held him firmly and stroked his back. Caruso settled himself and blinked his sparkling eyes. "Look at those golden red feathers. See these dark, green ones on his neck? This is a royal rooster, son! He's a champion!"

Uncle George pulled a cord from his pocket and tied it around Caruso's legs. "I hate to do this to you, Caruso, but you'll have a good master." He held the beautiful rooster out to me. I took him into my arms. I stroked his glowing feathers. "Caruso, Caruso, my Caruso," I said humbly.

I carried Caruso into the yard. I was ready to leave. "Be careful the foxes or hawks don't get Caruso now, son," Uncle George warned with a serious look on his bony face. "Or maybe a mink. Minks catch chickens, too," he said, walking me toward the gate.

"I'll take good care of him, Uncle George. I wouldn't take a thousand dollars for Caruso!" He held the gate shut. I fidgeted nervously. "Thank you for letting me have Caruso, Uncle George," I said, moving up to the gate.

Uncle George patted me on the back. "Be kind to Caruso, son." He stroked Caruso's feathers tenderly once more. "He's the grandest chicken Fanny and I ever raised. You are a good little worker, son. Come back sometime when I'm not busy and we'll go fishing."

"I will, Uncle George." I put my hand beside his on the gate and opened it slightly.

He opened the gate wider. "Now, be careful about the varmints. They'll catch Caruso if you don't watch out for him."

"I'll take care of him, Uncle George," I promised. He stood watching as I trotted down the lane. Caruso nestled in my arms. He held his head high, watchfully.

Dark shadows fell over Caruso and me. Light filtered through openings of moving objects. "A cloud," I thought, "is covering the sky. No, it moves close and low." I heard harsh sounds. They seemed to be calling, "Haw—Haw—Haw—" Objects floated low above us. "Haw — Haw — Haw — " They squawked and cried loudly close above my head.

"Hawks! Hawks, Caruso, that's what they are. What shall we do?" I ran toward the woods to shelter him. "Faster, Caruso, faster," I cried tiredly, as I hid in the darkness of the woods.

"Haw — Haw — Haw — " The hawks screamed at us. They followed us into the woods. I listened breathlessly as the big birds flew into the trees and continued their horrid "Haw — Haw — Haw —." I knew they must be collecting in great numbers to swoop down and snatch Caruso from me. I tucked him under my arm and crept silently into a narrow, hidden dark path, watching and hiding from the birds. My heart thumped and pounded. I panted and puffed.

I leaned my body forward and crept under a low-growing bush. I waited quietly until more darkness came. Then I tiptoed softly through dead leaves and limbs. A dry twig shattered loudly under my foot. I froze with fright. Caruso moved close to my body. He made no sound. The earth was deathly silent around us.

A dark figure appeared at the left of our dimly lit path. I sidled away into more low-growing shrubs and huddled against a decayed tree trunk to avoid the creature.

A bear? A wildcat? Or a ghost? "Haw — Haw — Haw — Haw — " now screamed at us from low-hanging limbs. The dark object remained still, blocking our way, ready to snatch Caruso from my arms as we passed — or maybe to grab both of us. I hunkered down on my knees and elbows, turning my back to the birds, shielding Caruso with my body. We would steal away from the bear, wildcat, or ghost when I caught my breath. The "Haw — Haw — Haw — " became slow, softly rhythmic, faintly dying away.

The darkening woods around us became still, except for the breathing of Caruso and me. I cried and whimpered as full darkness crept slowly over the woods. My tired legs ached. My chest pained and heaved. I held Caruso firmly and sank in the bedded leaves to rest. Tears filled my eyes. I felt that we would be swallowed by the monster, that Grandma and Grandpa would never get to see my beautiful rooster.

The ghostly crescent moon slipped quietly through fluffy clouds and half lighted our path. I held Caruso near my body and made ready to sneak past the scary creature, unseen. The earth around us remained deathly still other. than the quiet "hu — hu — hu — " of Caruso's breathing. He seemed to share my feeling of danger. Through tears, I searched for the dark figure that had blocked our path. It was no longer there. In the direction of where it had crouched, near Caruso and me, the outline of an animal with fire-like eyes stared at us. The piercing eyes moved stealthily toward Caruso.

I screamed! Caruso squalled! The birds above and around us cried loudly, "Haw! Haw! Haw!" One directly over us flipped and flopped, beating its wings against limbs and leaves. It fluttered noisily to the ground within inches of Caruso, crying and squalling, "Haw! Haw! Haw!" I jumped to my feet and held Caruso in my arms. The monster with the fiery eyes slunk slowly into the darkness. Quickly, I found our path and ran toward Grandpa's until I was out of breath. Now the woods lay far behind us!

Soon, we saw the light from Grandpa's window. I sighed happily, "We made it, Caruso! We made it."

Old Jack met us in the yard. He wagged his tail and licked my hand. I felt safe and secure. I pulled the latch on the kitchen door and called bravely, "I'm home, Grandpa! I'm home!"

"Come in, boy! We've been looking for you!" he answered, cheerfully.

"Look what I bought from Uncle George! He's mine!" I puffed and panted, holding Caruso up to Grandma in full light.

"What a beautiful rooster!" she said, stroking his wide back. "He's a nice one and just what we need —a rooster. I haven't had one with my hens for some time."

"I love Caruso, Grandma. Aunt Fanny named him before she died." I untied the cord from his legs and rubbed them. "What will we do with him tonight, Grandma? Could he sleep by my bed? We can turn him out with the hens tomorrow."

"Oh, no! A rooster wants to be with his hens." I could see that Grandma liked Caruso. "Just take him to the chicken house and set him on the roost beside one of the domernicker hens."

"A hundred or a thousand old black hawks tried to snatch Caruso out of my arms and carry him away, Grandpa. They flew right down over us and hollered 'Haw — Haw — Haw.' And a wildcat, a bear, or ghost tried to get us, too."

Grandpa smiled, "I don't know about the wildcat and the ghost, son. It was probably a hungry fox. There is nothing a fox likes more than a fine chicken. And those birds were not hawks. They were crows. Hawks are brownish, and they usually fly alone. Crows are black and they say, 'Caw — Caw — Caw.'"

Grandpa took Caruso into his hands and examined the muscles of the rooster's back and the tendons of his strong legs. "Ten crows couldn't whip your rooster, son. This is a fighting cock!" He held Caruso close. "Feel those sharp spurs! He'd tussle a hawk unless the hawk swooped down and caught him napping!"

"No hawk will catch Caruso napping, Grandpa.

No, sir. He's always up and crowing before daylight. A hawk won't find him asleep."

Grandma rose and started toward the kitchen. "I'll set your supper on the table while you put Caruso on the roost for the night." She hugged me as she passed. "A growing boy has to eat," she said.

I lit the lantern, carried Caruso to the henhouse, and set him on the roost beside a large hen. Then I walked back to the door, opening and closing it quietly. The small door through which Grandma's chickens went in and out was left open. As I walked along the path toward the house, I heard Caruso squawk loudly as he had when he saw the hawk. I supposed he was having a bad dream.

I went to bed happy, and I dreamed of *my* beautiful rooster. At the height of my dream, Grandpa shook me gently. "Get up, son, it's time to see about your rooster," he said. I jumped out of bed, pulled on my overalls, and dashed to the henhouse.

Grandma's hens were clucking noisily, picking at bugs and worms. I looked for Caruso. I listened for his "Cock-a-doodle-doo-o!" I ran into and around the chicken shed. I looked in the barn and the field around it. There was no sign of my beautiful Caruso!

I ran to the house. "Grandma, Grandma! My rooster is gone! My rooster is gone!" I cried. "My beautiful Caruso is gone! What shall we do, Grandpa?" I sobbed with disappointment.

"Calm yourself, son, calm yourself," he said, trying to console me. "We'll take Old Jack to the woods after breakfast and find that rooster. He's probably gone back to George's. We'll find him for you. Jack will follow his trail. We'll find him."

I ate hurriedly. After what I thought was an eternally long breakfast, we took the old dog to the edge of the woods and ordered him, "Sic 'im, Jack! Go get 'im, Jack! Go find the rooster." We commanded him over and over. We coaxed and scolded, but Jack didn't budge.

"Could your rooster fly, son?" Grandpa asked.

"Oh, yes. He flew on high posts and crowed at Uncle George's."

"Then he's flown through the trees leaving Jack no trail to follow. Let's go to George's. That's where we'll find him."

We hurried to Uncle George's. "No," said Uncle George, "Caruso hasn't shown himself here!" He scowled, "Ma should have known better than turn Caruso loose so soon." He bit his lip and dug the toe of his shoe into the dirt. "Poor Caruso," he said, sadly. "Fanny's Caruso is a goner."

We looked around the chicken house, in the barn, through the fields and woods. We saw other chickens, but not the beautiful Caruso.

Uncle George said mournfully, "The varmints, maybe a fox or a hawk, caught Caruso. That's what's happened to him!" He pointed to a lone, large bird sailing overhead. "One of those long-tailed, copper-colored hawks swooped right down here in the chicken yard and caught one of my fat hens."

"No hawk got him, George. He was in the woods. If anything, a fox has carried him to his den," Grandpa said.

"Caruso is still alive, and I'll find him," I insisted. It was only midsummer. I had another month to stay in the country.

Each morning I went into the woods and fields, seeking my Caruso. "Chick, chick, chick. Here, Caruso. Here, Caruso. Here, boy. Come to me, Caruso," I would call.

Grandma and Grandpa tried to console me. "We'll go to George's and get the finest young rooster he has and have it here for you when you come back next summer," they promised.

"But I want Caruso. He was the best rooster in the whole wide world," I protested. "I only want Caruso."

The thought of a varmint killing and eating my Caruso made me furious. "Let's go kill all the foxes and hawks. If we don't hurry, they'll be sure to catch Caruso," I pleaded. "Let's go!"

"No, son," Grandpa said. "I need them. If it weren't for the foxes and hawks, other animals — like rats, mice, and rabbits — would eat up every grain of corn, every head of cabbage, and every blade of grass on the farm. We need some varmints to catch other harmful pests."

"I see," I said. "But we don't need the ones that are after Caruso," I argued. I wanted to agree with Grandpa. Yet I felt he had deserted me and was no longer interested in finding my rooster. I went to the barn, climbed up into the hayloft, and cried until Grandma rang the bell for supper. Old Jack waited for me and wagged his tail when I climbed down. He was the only friend I had left, I felt.

It was the last week that I was to stay in the country. "So you haven't seen feather nor spur of Caruso?" Uncle George asked on his regular Sunday visits. "You might as well give up and forget Caruso, son. He's a goner for sure. One of those big copper-colored hawks caught him."

But none of their talk defeated me. I would continue to look for my Caruso.

The afternoon before I was to leave, I called Old Jack. "Let's go to Johnson's Meadow over beyond the woods, Jack. Maybe Caruso went in the wrong direction. Maybe he left before daylight and got lost."

Jack seemed to understand. He ran on ahead. He sniffed along zigzagging trails through tall grass and high weeds. We crossed the stream that fed our swimming hole. We climbed a low fence. We walked through thick, dark woods and out into the open pasture.

"Caruso must be gone forever, Jack. We better go, too," I said. Then, something seemed to say to me, "Over that rise — over that rise."

I felt myself being pulled and lifted toward a little hill.

I called, "Come on, Jack! Let's go!" Jack followed me as I ran toward the top of the low hill. I just about flew the last few yards near the summit. I stopped and looked down. I saw a dark object. I knew that I had found Caruso, my beautiful rooster.  There, among the bright purple and yellow feathers from his wings and breast, was a sweeping golden green one from his tail. I ran to it. I picked it up. "Oh," I cried. "My Caruso. My poor Caruso. My beautiful Caruso." My eyes filled. I blubbered, "Caruso, Caruso, Caruso."

I held the feather tenderly and stroked it as I had stroked his strong body. It curved like a beautiful rainbow. I stood fascinated. I turned to leave. Then I saw feathers that did not come from Caruso. They were strewn over an area larger than where his feathers had been. They were long, copper-colored ones from the tail of more than one hawk.

"You didn't swoop down and find *my* Caruso napping, old hawks," I said, shaking my fist at the shadow of a lone large bird passing overhead. "It took more than one of you to catch my Caruso," I bragged. I hurried home.

"Look, Grandpa! Look!" I shouted. "I found Caruso!" I held the beautiful feather high. "Those old copper-colored hawks caught him, but he gave them a good tussle. See? See these feathers?" I pulled two long copper-colored feathers from my pocket. I threw the hateful hawk feathers into the trash pile. "There! There!" I said angrily. "Caruso flogged and fought you, too."

Grandma came from the kitchen. I ran to her. "See? See, Grandma?" I whimpered. "Those old hawks caught him." I burst into tears.

Grandma pulled me close. "Now, now, everything will be all right," she said, soothingly. "Everything will be all right, son."

I placed the beautiful feather in her hand. "Give it to Uncle George, Grandma. It will help him remember Aunt Fanny's Caruso. Caruso was never really mine." I sobbed and cried quietly.

A little while later, Grandpa placed his arm around my shoulders. Together we walked out the door toward our swimming hole under the railroad trestle.

"I'll always remember Caruso, Grandpa."

"Yes," said Grandpa. "I know. I know."

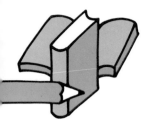

When Clouds Cry

Imagine that you have just heard a weather report. The reporter might have said, "It rained today." But suppose the reporter had said, "The clouds cried today." That kind of report would seem very unusual. You know that clouds don't cry. Only people cry. The unusual report had talked about clouds as though they were people. The reporter had used personification to describe the weather.

Personification is a way of using language that makes a thing seem like a person. In personification, a thing is described as acting or speaking like a person.

Writers use personification for special reasons. They may want to paint an interesting picture in the reader's mind. They may want to describe something in a new and different way. The use of personification often makes writing stronger and more interesting that it would be otherwise.

There are examples of personification in the story "My Caruso." One sentence reads: "Tall corn slapped and beat his face." In this sentence, the corn is described as though it were an angry person hitting someone. By using personification, the writer has created a very clear picture of the way the boy felt as he moved through the rows of corn.

ACTIVITY A   Read the sentence that is an example
of personification. Then read the three sentences
that follow. Choose the sentence that correctly
explains the meaning of the personification example.
Write that sentence on your paper.

1. The maple tree wears its new leaves proudly.
   a. The tree is like a person laughing loudly.
   b. The tree is like a person dressed in
      new clothes.
   c. The tree is like a person running away.

2. The wind races furiously to the sea.
   a. The wind is like an angry person running.
   b. The wind is like a person who feels ill.
   c. The wind is like a person singing sadly.

3. The walls of the office hear many sad tales.
   a. The walls are like a person talking softly.
   b. The walls are like a person writing a note.
   c. The walls are like a person who hears
      unhappy stories.

ACTIVITY B   Read each sentence that is an example
of personification. Decide what kind of person you
think of when you read the sentence. Use this form
to write your answer on your paper: The _____ is
like a person _____ .

1. The thunder shouts in anger to the ground below.
2. The moon hides shyly behind a row of clouds.
3. The morning sun awakens and yawns in the sky.

HAPPENINGS

Everything that happens to you helps make you the special person you are. In "Happenings," you read about the experiences of several different characters and how each character changed in some way. Perhaps you've learned a few things from reading about these happenings. Perhaps you've begun to realize that we can learn and grow from our experiences.

Thinking About "Happenings"

1. What is one important thing that Wilbur learns from Charlotte?
2. Why did Rudy Soto finally let the hawk go?
3. What things happened to Wufu that helped her to grow up?
4. What are some things that the boys in "My Caruso" and "Hawk, I'm Your Brother" learned from their experiences with their pets?
5. Which story did you like best? Why?
6. If you were the author of "My Caruso" how would you end the story? Write a paragraph describing your ending.

Glossary

This glossary will help you to pronounce and to understand the meanings of some of the unusual or difficult words in this book.

The pronunciation of each word is printed beside the word in this way: **o·pen** (ō′pən). The letters, signs, and key words in the list below will help you read the pronunciation respelling. When an entry word has more than one syllable, a dark accent mark (′) is placed after the syllable that has the heaviest stress. In some words, a light accent mark (′) is placed after the syllable that receives a less heavy stress.

The pronunciation key, syllable breaks, accent mark placements, and phonetic respellings in this glossary are adapted from the Macmillan *School Dictionary* (1981) and the Macmillan *Dictionary* (1981). Other dictionaries may use other pronunciation symbols.

Pronunciation Key

a	bad	**hw**	white	**ô**	off	**th**	that	**ə**	*stands for*
ā	cake	**i**	it	**oo**	wood	**u**	cup	a	*as in* ago
ä	father	**ī**	ice	**ōo**	food	**ur**	turn	e	*as in* taken
b	bat	**j**	joke	**oi**	oil	**yōo**	music	i	*as in* pencil
ch	chin	**k**	kit	**ou**	out	**v**	very	o	*as in* lemon
d	dog	**l**	lid	**p**	pail	**w**	wet	u	*as in* helpful
e	pet	**m**	man	**r**	ride	**y**	yes		
ē	me	**n**	not	**s**	sit	**z**	zoo		
f	five	**ng**	sing	**sh**	ship	**zh**	treasure		
g	game	**o**	hot	**t**	tall				
h	hit	**ō**	open	**th**	thin				

A

at · tach · ment (ə tach′mənt) *n.*   a part or device that is connected to a larger thing.

B

beech · nut (bēch′nut′) *n.*   the nut of the beech tree, used to make cooking oil and flavoring.

bin (bin) *n.*   a closed place or box for holding something.

boast (bōst) *v.*   to talk too much or with too much pride about oneself; brag. — *n.*   a thing boasted of; a cause for pride.

bog (bog) *n.*   wet, spongy ground; marsh; swamp.

bolt up · right (bōlt up′rīt′)   stiffly straight; erect.

breast (brest) *n.*   the front part of the body.

bulb (bulb) *n.*   a round, underground part of a plant. Plants such as tulips, onions, and lilies grow from bulbs.

bur · row (bur′ō) *v.*   to dig a hole in the ground.

C

cac · tus wren (kak′təs ren′) a small songbird that makes its nest in a cactus.

Ca · ru · so (kə rōo′ sō)

cat · tail (kat′tāl) *n.*   a tall plant that grows in marshes. Cattails have long, furry brown tips.

cattail

cau · tious · ly (kô′ shəs lē) *adv.*   very carefully.

Ca · vat · i · ca (kə vat′ə kə)

chir · rup (chēr′əp, chur′əp) *v.*   to chirp continuously.

cho · rus (kôr′əs) *n.*   a group of people who sing or dance together.

clus · ter (klus′tər) *n.*   a number of things of the same kind that grow or are grouped together.

comb (kōm) *n.*   a thick, fleshy crest on the head of roosters and other fowl.

con · quer · or (kong′kər ər) *n.*   a person who overcomes or defeats another person or other persons.

con · sole (kən sōl′) *v.*   to comfort.

corn · crib (kôrn′krib′) *n.*   a bin or small building for storing cobs of corn, built with slats that are spaced for ventilation.

court · ship (kôrt′ship′) *n.*   a courting; wooing.

cox · a (kok′sə) *n.*   the first segment of the leg of an insect.

cray · fish (krā′fish′) *n.*   a small freshwater animal that looks something like a lobster.

cres · cent (kres′ənt) *adj.*   shaped like the moon when it appears thin and curved.

crouch (krouch) *v.*   to stoop or bend low with the knees bent.

cur · lew (kur′lōo) *n.*   a wading bird of arctic and temperate regions.

crescent

D

de · cay (di kā′) *v.*   to rot slowly.

de · lec · ta · ble (di lek′tə bəl) *adj.*   highly pleasing, especially to the taste.

dog · wood (dog′wood′) *n.* a tree that has flowers with a greenish-yellow center and pink or white leaves that look like petals.

doze (dōz) *v.* to sleep lightly or for a short time.

drag · line (drag′līn′) *n.* a dragrope or guide rope.

E

ee · rie (ēr′ē) *adj.* strange in a scary way; making people frightened or nervous.

e · las · tic (i las′tik) *adj.* able to go back to the same shape soon after being stretched, squeezed, or pressed.

en · chant (en chant′) *v.* **1.** to charm. **2.** to bewitch.

en · e · my (en′ə mē) *n.* a person, animal or thing that is dangerous or harmful.

e · ter · nal · ly (i turn′ə lē) *adv.* always; for all time; without stopping.

ex · am · ine (eg zam′in) *v.* to look at closely and carefully; check.

F

farm · hand (färm′hand′) *n.* a person who works on a farm.

fas · ci · nate (fas′ə nāt′) *v.* to attract and hold the interest of; charm.

fe · mur (fē′mər) *n.* the long bone of the upper leg; thigh bone.

fidg · et (fij′it) *v.* to be nervous or uneasy; to make restless movements.

fil · ter (fil′tər) *v.* to go through slowly.

flick (flik) *v.* to hit or remove with a quick, light snap.

flog (flog) *v.* **flogged, flog · ging.** to beat or whip severely.

fore · arm (fôr′ärm′) *n.* the part of the arm between the elbow and the wrist.

fret (fret) *v.* to be upset, or worried.

fur · ther · more (fur′thər môr′) *adv.* in addition; moreover, besides.

G

ge · ra · ni · um (jə rā′nē əm) *n.* a plant with bright red, pink, or white flowers.

glum (glum) *adj.* gloomy.

gos · ling (goz′ling) *n.* a young goose.

gra · cious · ly (grā′shəs lē) *adv.* in a graceful and charming manner.

geranium

gram · o · phone (gram′ə fōn′) *n.* a phonograph.

grub (grub) *n.* a beetle or other insect in any early stage of growth, when it looks like a worm.

H

half hitch (haf′hich′) a knot made by passing the end of a rope around the rope and then through the loop thus made.

---

a bad, ā cake, ä father; e pet, ē me; i it, ī ice; o hot, ō open, ô off; oo wood, ōō food; oi oil, ou out; th thin, th that; u cup, ur turn, yōō music; zh treasure; ə ago, taken, pencil, lemon, helpful

hawk (hôk) *n.*   a bird of prey. A hawk has a sharp, hooked beak, long claws, and short rounded wings.

hawk

hay · fork (hā'fôrk') *n.* a pitchfork.

hay · loft (hā'lôft') *n.* a loft, or upper story, in a barn or stable for storing hay.

her · mit thrush (hur'mit thrush') a bird with a brown body, a spotted breast, and a reddish-brown tail.

hi · ber · na · tion (hī'bər nā'shən) *n.* spending the winter in a dormant or in-active state, as do many animals, such as bears, squirrels, and snakes.

ho · ri · zon (hə rī'zən) *n.*   the line where the sky and the ground or the sea seem to meet.

hum · bly (hum'blē) *adv.*   in a way that is not proud.

hun · ker (hun'kər) *v.*   to squat.

I

in · ter · rupt (in'tə rupt') *v.*   to break in upon or stop a person who is acting or speaking.

K

kind · ling (kind'ling) *n.*   material for starting a fire, especially small pieces of wood.

knob (nob) *n.*   a rounded lump.

know-how (nō'hou') *n.*   the knowledge of how to do something; practical skill.

L

lac · y (lā'sē) *adj.*   of or resembling lace.

la · dy · bird (lā'dē burd') *n.*   a lady-bug; a small round insect that is red or orange with black spots.

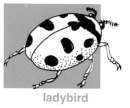
ladybird

leath · er · y (leth̶'ər ē) *adj.*   like leather; tough and hardened.

lone · li · ness (lōn'lē nəs) *n.*   the state or quality of being lonely.

M

man · ure (mə noor', mə nyoor') *n.*   waste matter from animals that is used to fertilize land.

marsh · y bog (märsh'ē bog')   low, wet, soft land covered with grasses and reeds.

mel · on (mel'ən) *n.*   a large fruit that grows on a vine. Mel-ons have a sweet, soft pulp that can be eaten.

mem · brane (mem'brān) *n.*   a thin layer of skin or tissue.

melon

met · a · tar · sus (met'ə tär'səs) *n.* the part of the foot between the ankle and the toes, consisting of five bones.

mim · ic (mim'ik) *v.* **mim · icked, mim · ick · ing.**   to imitate; copy movement or sound.

moth (môth) *n.*   an insect that looks like a butterfly, but that flies mostly at night. The larvae of some moths eat holes in wool and other fabrics.

moun · tain · side (mount'ən sīd') *n.*   the side or slope of a mountain.

mourn · ful · ly (môrn'fə lē) *adv.*   in a manner expressing sorrow.

mus · ty (mus'tē) *adj.*   moldy; stale.

N

nerv · ous · ly (nur'vəs lē) *adv.*   uneasily; anxiously.

O

ob · lige (ə blīj') *v.*   to make thankful for a service or a favor.

P

par · tic · u · lar (pər tik'yə lər) *adj.*   very careful; special.

pa · tel · la (pə tel'ə) *n.*   the kneecap.

per · suade (pər swād') *v.*   to cause to do or believe something by argument; convince.

pest (pest) *n.*   a person or thing that is troublesome or annoying; nuisance.

pierc · ing (pēr'sing) *adj.*   sharp and shrill.

pin · point (pin'point') *n.*   **1.** the point of a pin. **2.** something very small or unimportant.

pip · er (pī'pər) *n.*   a person who plays on a pipe, especially a bagpipe.

plead (plēd) *v.*   to request; beg.

plo · ver (pluv'ər, plō'vər) *n.*   a bird with a straight, pointed bill.

pos · sum (pos'əm) *n.*   a small furry animal. The female carries its young in a pouch on its stomach. This animal is usually called an *opossum.*

prey (prā) *n.*   an animal that is hunted by another animal for food.

pug nose (pug' nōz)   a short, broad, turned-up nose.

pul · let (pool'it) *n.*   a young hen less than a year old.

Q

Queens · bor · o Bridge (kwēnz'bər ō)   a bridge in New York City over the East River, connecting the borough of Manhattan to the borough of Queens.

ques · tion · ing · ly (kwes'chə ning lē) *adv.*   in the manner of one who questions.

R

rac · coon (ra'kōōn') *n.*   a small animal with brownish-gray fur. It has a pointed face with black mask-like markings and a long, bushy tail marked with black rings.

raccoon

raft · er (raf'tər) *n.*   one of the sloping beams that support a roof.

---

a bad, ā cake, ä father; e pet, ē me; i it, ī ice; o hot, ō open, ô off; oo wood, ōō food; oi oil, ou out; th thin, <u>th</u> that; u cup, ur turn, yōō music; zh treasure; ə ago, taken, pencil, lemon, helpful

rail · road tres · tle (rāl′rōd′ tres′əl) a framework used to support a railroad bridge.

re · build (rē bild′) v. **re · built, re · build · ing. 1.** to build again. **2.** to make changes in, repair, or remodel.

reed (rēd) n. a tall grass having long, narrow leaves and jointed stems.

re · mark · a · ble (ri mär′kə bəl) adj. worthy of being noticed; not ordinary, unusual.

rhyth · mic (ri<u>th</u>′mic) adj. having a regular or orderly repetition of sounds or movement.

roost (rōōst) n. a perch on which birds rest or sleep.

S

scal · lop (skol′əp, skal′əp) v. to shape or make with a series of curves.

sed · en · tar · y (sed′ən ter′ē) adj. remaining in one place, not moving about.

sen · si · tive (sen′sə tiv) adj. capable of receiving signals through the senses.

se · ries (sēr′ēz) n. a number of similar things coming one after another.

shear (shēr) v. to cut off; remove.

si · dle (sīd′əl) v. to move sideways, especially in a sly manner.

sil · hou · ette (sil′ōō et′) n. a picture or drawing showing the outline of a figure or object filled in with black or another solid color.

snag (snag) v. to catch by a quick action.

snail (snāl) n. a kind of animal that is found in water and on land. Snails have soft bodies that are protected by a spiral-shaped shell.

snif · fle (snif′əl) v. to breathe through the nose or sniff again and again.

sod (sod) n. the top layer of soil that has grass growing on it.

spin · ner · et (spin′ə ret′) n. an organ by which various animals, such as spiders, spin silken threads.

spur (spur) n. a spine-like projection on the legs of certain birds.

squall (skwôl) v. to cry or scream loudly and harshly.

stag · ger (stag′ər) v. to move or cause to move with a swaying motion.

stale (stāl) adj. **1.** not fresh. **2.** not new or interesting.

steal · thi · ly (stel′thə lē) adv. in a secret manner.

sum · mit (sum′it) n. the highest point.

sun · down (sun′ doun′) n. the setting of the sun.

sur · face (sur′fis) n. the outside or top part of a thing.

swal · low (swol′ō) n. a small bird with long wings and a forked tail.

T

tar · di · ness (tär′dē nəs) n. lateness.

tar · sus (tär′səs) n. the seven small bones making up the ankle.

task (task) n. a piece of work to be done.

tempt · ing (temp′ting) adj. attractive; appealing.

tex · ture (teks′chər) n. the look or feel of something.

tib · i · a (tib′ē ə) n. the inner and thicker of the two bones of the leg, extending from the knee to the ankle; shinbone.

trick · le (trik′ əl) v. to flow or fall drop by drop or in a thin stream.

trill (tril) *n.* a quavering, trembling, usually high-pitched sound.

tro · chan · ter (trō kan′tər) *n.* any of several jutting processes at the upper end of the thighbone.

trough (trôf) *n.* a long, deep, narrow box or other container. Farmers use troughs to hold food and water for animals.

truf · fle (truf′əl) *n.* a mushroom shaped like a potato that grows underground.

tus · sle (tus′əl) *v.* to engage in a disorderly fight.

twitch (twich) *v.* to move or pull with a sudden jerk or tug.

U

un · har · ness (un här′nis) *v.* to take the harness or gear from.

V

vague · ly (vāg′lē) *adv.* not in a clear or definite manner.

var · mint (vär′mint) *n.* a troublesome or objectionable animal or person.

vel · vet (vel′vit) *n.* a fabric with soft, thick pile.

vi · bra · tion (vī brā′ shən) *n.* rapid movement back and forth or up and down.

W

wat · tle (wot′əl) *n.* the fleshy, often brightly colored fold of skin hanging down from the neck or throat of certain birds.

whif · fle tree (hwif′əl trē′) the pivoted crossbar at the front of a wagon or carriage to which the traces of the harness are attached.

whip · poor · will (hwip′ər wil′) *n.* **1.** a plump bird of eastern North America, active at night. **2.** the call of this bird.

whirl · wind (whurl′wind′) *n.* a rapidly or violently rotating column of air.

wit · ness (wit′nis) *v.* to be present to see or hear something.

woo · ing (wo̅o̅′ing) *n.* seeking the love and affection of someone, usually with the intent to marry.

Wu · fu (wo̅o̅′fo̅o̅)

Z

zig · zag (zig′zag′) *v.* **zig · zagged, zig · zag · ging.** to move in a line, pattern, or course that has a series of short, sharp turns from side to side.

a bad, ā cake, ä father; e pet, ē me; i it, ī ice; o hot, ō open, ô off; oo wood, o̅o̅ food; oi oil, ou out; th thin, th that; u cup, ur turn, yo̅o̅ music; zh treasure; ə ago, taken, pencil, lemon, helpful